SCIENCE STARTERS
Sound

by Carolyn Bernhardt

BELLWETHER MEDIA • MINNEAPOLIS, MN

Note to Librarians, Teachers, and Parents:

Blastoff! Readers are carefully developed by literacy experts and combine standards-based content with developmentally appropriate text.

Level 1 provides the most support through repetition of high-frequency words, light text, predictable sentence patterns, and strong visual support.

Level 2 offers early readers a bit more challenge through varied simple sentences, increased text load, and less repetition of high-frequency words.

Level 3 advances early-fluent readers toward fluency through increased text and concept load, less reliance on visuals, longer sentences, and more literary language.

Level 4 builds reading stamina by providing more text per page, increased use of punctuation, greater variation in sentence patterns, and increasingly challenging vocabulary.

Level 5 encourages children to move from "learning to read" to "reading to learn" by providing even more text, varied writing styles, and less familiar topics.

Whichever book is right for your reader, Blastoff! Readers are the perfect books to build confidence and encourage a love of reading that will last a lifetime!

This edition first published in 2019 by Bellwether Media, Inc.

No part of this publication may be reproduced in whole or in part without written permission of the publisher. For information regarding permission, write to Bellwether Media, Inc., Attention: Permissions Department, 6012 Blue Circle Drive, Minnetonka, MN 55343.

Library of Congress Cataloging-in-Publication Data

Names: Bernhardt, Carolyn, author.
Title: Sound / by Carolyn Bernhardt.
Description: Minneapolis, MN : Bellwether Media, Inc., 2019. | Series: Blastoff! Readers. Science Starters | Includes bibliographical references and index. | Audience: 5-8. | Audience: K to 3.
Identifiers: LCCN 2017061623 (print) | LCCN 2018009252 (ebook) | ISBN 9781681035444 (ebook) | ISBN 9781626178113 (hardcover ; alk. paper) | ISBN 9781618914675 (pbk. ; alk. paper)
Subjects: LCSH: Sound–Juvenile literature. | Sound–Measurement–Juvenile literature.
Classification: LCC QC225.5 (ebook) | LCC QC225.5 .B53 2019 (print) | DDC 534–dc23
LC record available at https://lccn.loc.gov/2017061623

Text copyright © 2019 by Bellwether Media, Inc. BLASTOFF! READERS and associated logos are trademarks and/or registered trademarks of Bellwether Media, Inc. SCHOLASTIC, CHILDREN'S PRESS, and associated logos are trademarks and/or registered trademarks of Scholastic Inc., 557 Broadway, New York, NY 10012.

Editor: Christina Leaf   Designer: Josh Brink

Printed in the United States of America, North Mankato, MN

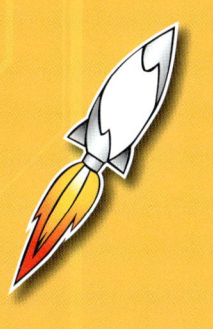

Table of Contents

The Speed of Sound   4
What Is Sound?   6
Hearing   10
Volume and Pitch   12
Echoes and Echolocation   16
Musical Sounds   20
Glossary   22
To Learn More   23
Index   24

The Speed of Sound

You watch the swimmers step onto their starting blocks. Then, "BEEP!" They take off.

You hear the splash as they dive in. The crowd cheers. Sound can quickly set things into motion!

What Is Sound?

sound waves

Sounds are **vibrations** that touch our ears so we can hear. Sounds travel in waves called **sound waves**.

Sound waves form when something vibrates. They are made up of **energy**.

vibration

Sound needs a **medium** to travel through. Mediums can be air, water, or solid objects such as doors or walls.

solid medium

Sound travels fastest through solids and slowest through gases.

Hearing

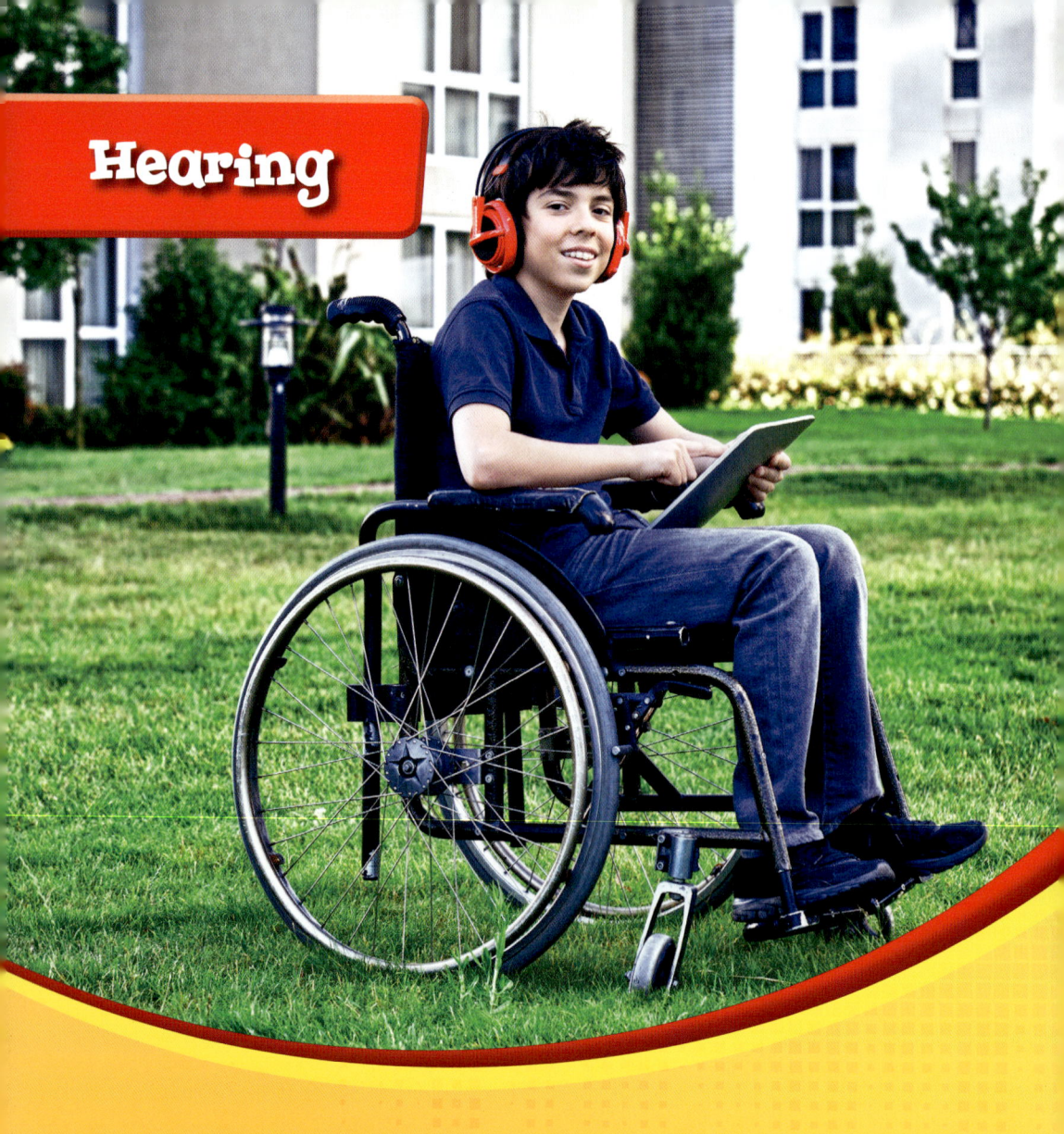

We hear things when sound waves reach our ears. Inside each ear is a thin layer of skin called an **eardrum**. It vibrates when a sound wave touches it.

Our ears send **signals** to our brains so we can understand what we hear.

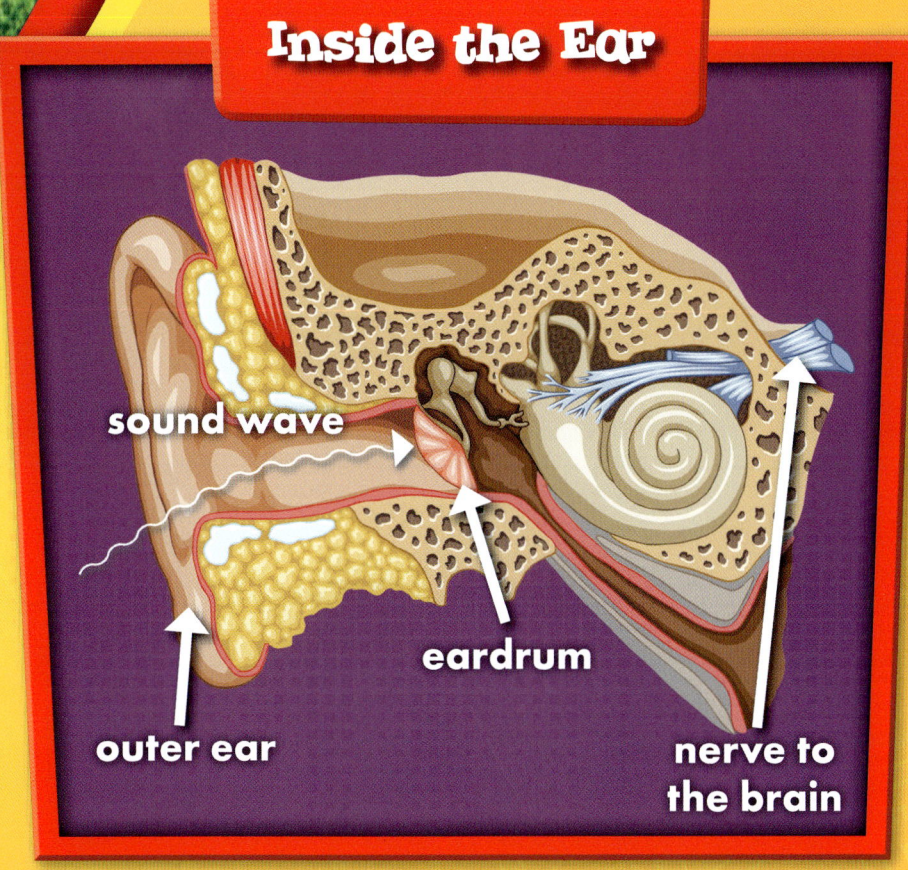

Inside the Ear

sound wave

outer ear

eardrum

nerve to the brain

Volume and Pitch

A sound wave's **amplitude** makes a sound loud or soft. This is volume.

12

Amplitude and Volume

quieter   louder

amplitude

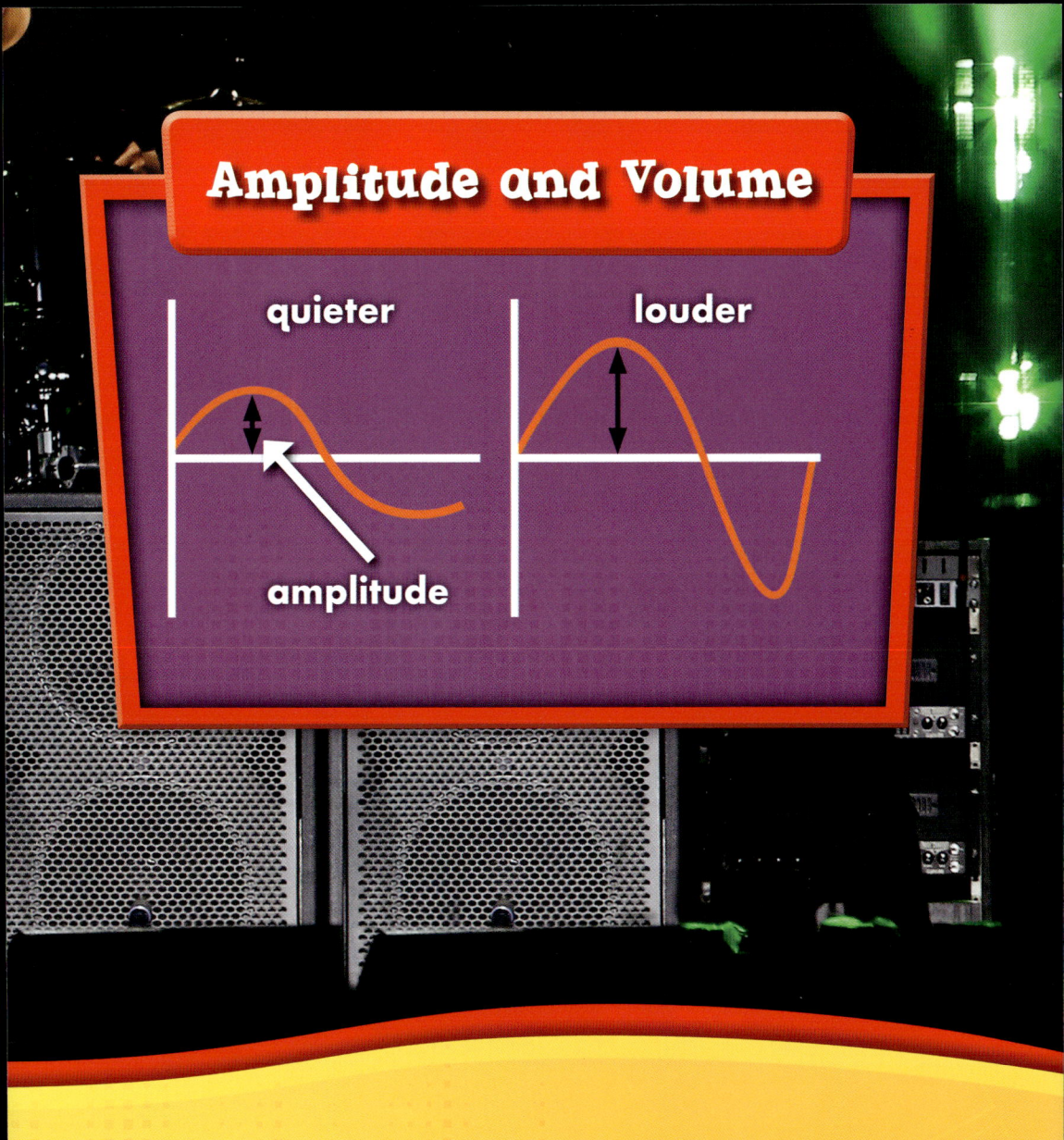

Sound waves with big amplitudes carry more energy. This makes sounds louder because they push harder on our eardrums. Small amplitudes make quieter sounds.

13

Sounds have different **frequencies** based on the speed of vibration. The frequency makes a sound's **pitch**.

Higher frequencies make high-pitched sounds. Lower frequencies make low-pitched sounds. Some pitches are too high or low for the human ear to hear!

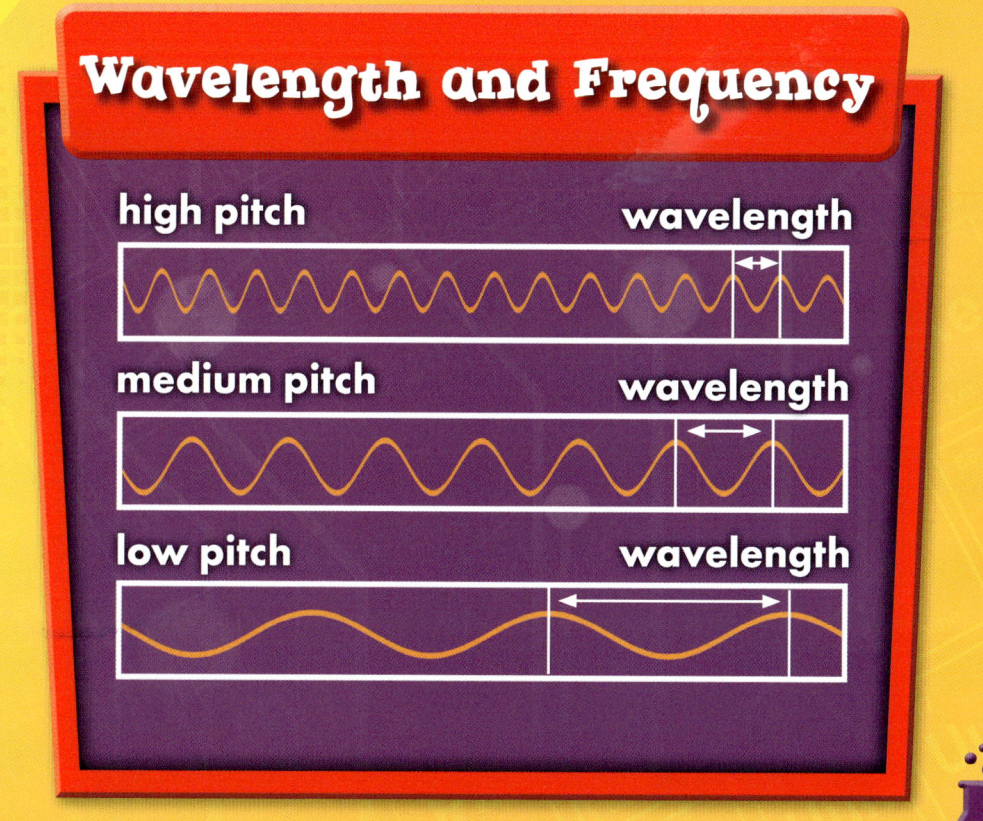

Wavelength and Frequency

high pitch — wavelength

medium pitch — wavelength

low pitch — wavelength

Echoes and Echolocation

Sometimes sound waves hit something and bounce back. This **reflection** of sound is an **echo**.

Sound bounces off of hard, smooth surfaces best. Softer surfaces soak up the sound's energy so it cannot travel any further or bounce back.

Some animals use sound to hunt and move around safely. This is called **echolocation**. Bats, dolphins, and some whales echolocate.

Echolocation

sound =)   echo = (

Animals that echolocate throw out sound and listen. The echo tells them how far away food and other objects are.

19

Musical Sounds

Instruments are made of many materials, including wood, brass, and strings. These materials all vibrate differently when they are played. They create different sounds that work together to make music!

Make an Instrument

You can see sound waves in action with this rubber band instrument!

What you will need:
- a rubber band
- a box
- two markers

1. Stretch the rubber band around the box.
2. Place the markers 2 inches (5 centimeters) apart under the rubber band. Strum the rubber band and listen to the sound it makes.
3. Pull the markers farther apart and strum the band. What happens to the pitch of the sound? Is it higher or lower?
4. Keep pulling the markers farther apart to test the pitch. What do you notice?

Glossary

amplitude—the measurement of a wave from the middle to the edge

eardrum—a thin, tightly stretched piece of skin in the ear that vibrates when sound waves hit it

echo—a sound that is a reflection of another sound; echoes are produced when sound waves bounce off a surface.

echolocation—a process for finding objects by using reflected sound waves

energy—useable power that allows things to be active

frequencies—speeds at which sound waves vibrate; frequency creates pitch.

medium—a substance through which sound is carried

pitch—the highness or lowness of a sound

reflection—the return of light or sound waves from a surface

signals—messages to the brain

sound waves—waves that form when a sound is made; sound waves carry sound to your ear.

vibrations—the movements of something shaking back and forth

To Learn More

AT THE LIBRARY
Johnson, Robin. *What Are Sound Waves?* New York, N.Y.: Crabtree Publishing Company, 2014.

Kuskowski, Alex. *Science Experiments with Sight & Sound.* Minneapolis, Minn.: ABDO Pub. Company, 2014.

Lawrence, Ellen. *Sound.* New York, N.Y.: Bearport Publishing, 2014.

ON THE WEB
Learning more about sound is as easy as 1, 2, 3.

1. Go to www.factsurfer.com.

2. Enter "sound" into the search box.

3. Click the "Surf" button and you will see a list of related web sites.

With factsurfer.com, finding more information is just a click away.

Index

activity, 21
amplitude, 12, 13
brains, 11
cheers, 5
eardrum, 10, 11, 13
ears, 6, 10, 11, 15
echo, 16, 19
echolocation, 18, 19
energy, 7, 13, 17
frequencies, 14, 15
hear, 5, 6, 10, 11, 15
instruments, 20, 21
medium, 8, 9
music, 20
pitch, 14, 15

reflection, 16
signals, 11
sound waves, 6, 7, 10, 11, 12, 13, 16
splash, 5
swimmers, 4
vibrations, 6, 7, 10, 14, 20
volume, 12, 13

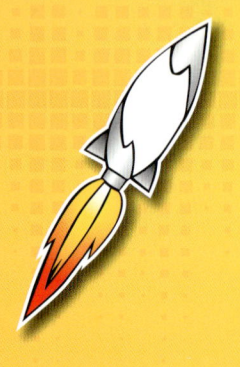

The images in this book are reproduced through the courtesy of: charobnica, front cover (periodic table); John Dakapu, front cover (circuit); By ADS Portrait, front cover (hero); Federico Rostango, p. 4; TORWAISTUDIO, p. 5; PrinceOfLove, p. 6; Trofimov Denis, p. 7; PR Image Factory, p. 8; Kamira, p. 9; baranozdemir, p. 10; Oguz Aral, p. 11; Debby Wong, pp. 12-13; John Roman Images, p. 14; stock_colors, p. 16; LuckyImages, p. 17; Andrea Izzotti, p. 18; Kong Vector, p. 19; Rapeepat Pornsipak, p. 20; Tamara JM Peterson, p. 21; ozanuysal, p. 24.